WHEN VEINS IGNITE

Abhijit Naskar is the twenty-first century Neuroscientist whose contributions in Cognitive and Behavioral Neuroscience have helped the world tackle the issues of mental illness, prejudice, hate, extremism, discrimination and segregation more effectively. As an untiring advocate of mental health and universal acceptance, he became a beloved best-selling author all over the world with his very first book "The Art of Neuroscience in Everything". With his pioneering ventures into the Neuropsychology of beliefs and biases, he has hugely contributed in the eradication of religious and cultural differences in our world, for which he is popularly hailed as the humanitarian scientist, who takes the human civilization in the path of sweet general harmony.

WHEN VEINS ignite

Either Integration or Degradation

ABHIJIT NASKAR

Also by Abhijit Naskar

The Art of Neuroscience in Everything
Your Own Neuron: A Tour of Your Psychic Brain
The God Parasite: Revelation of Neuroscience
The Spirituality Engine
Love Sutra: The Neuroscientific Manual of Love
Homo: A Brief History of Consciousness
Neurosutra: The Abhijit Naskar Collection
Autobiography of God: Biopsy of A Cognitive Reality
Biopsy of Religions: Neuroanalysis towards Universal
Tolerance
Prescription: Treating India's Soul
What is Mind?
In Search of Divinity: Journey to The Kingdom of Conscience
Love, God & Neurons: Memoir of a scientist who found
himself by getting lost
The Islamophobic Civilization: Voyage of Acceptance
Neurons of Jesus: Mind of A Teacher, Spouse & Thinker
Neurons, Oxygen & Nanak
The Education Decree
Principia Humanitas
The Krishna Cancer
Rowdy Buddha: The First Sapiens
We Are All Black: A Treatise on Racism
The Bengal Tigress: A Treatise on Gender Equality
Either Civilized or Phobic: A Treatise on Homosexuality
Wise Mating: A Treatise on Monogamy
Illusion of Religion: A Treatise on Religious
Fundamentalism
The Film Testament
Human Making is Our Mission: A Treatise on Parenting
I Am The Thread: My Mission
7 Billion Gods: Humans Above All
Lord is My Sheep: Gospel of Human
Morality Absolute
A Push in Perception
Let The Poor Be Your God
Conscience over Nonsense
Saint of The Sapiens
Time to Save Medicine
Fabric of Humanity

Build Bridges not Walls: In the name of Americana
The Constitution of The United Peoples of Earth
Lives to Serve Before I Sleep
When Humans Unite: Making A World Without Borders
All For Acceptance
Monk Meets World
Mission Reality
Citizens of Peace: Beyond The Savagery of Sovereignty
Operation Justice: To Make A Society That Needs No Law
See No Gender
The Gospel of Technology
Every Generation Needs Caretakers: The Gospel of
Patriotism
Aşkanjali: The Sufi Sermon
Mad About Humans: World Maker's Almanac
Revolution Indomable
When Call The People: My World My Responsibility
No Foreigner Only Family
Hurricane Humans: Give me accountability, I'll give you
peace
Ain't Enough to Look Human
Servitude is Sanctitude
Time To End Democracy: The Meritocratic Manifesto
I Vicdansaadet Speaking: No Rest Till The World is Lifted
Boldly Comes Justice: Sentient not Silent
Good Scientist: When Science and Service Combine
Sleepless for Society
Neden Türk: The Gospel of Secularism
Martyr Meets World: To Solve The Hard Problem of
Inhumanity
The Shape of A Human: Our America Their America

DEDICATION

To every human who believes in equality.

CONTENTS

1. Preamble

I Give You My Life
(The Sonnet)

I give you my life,
Crossing all foul insecurity.
Don't let me dwindle in chains,
Accept this offering of my serenity.
Pour me with all your suffering,
So I can bathe in your smile.
Take this torch of my burning soul,
With it light up your shadowy aisle.
Darkness is a fiendish illusion,
Our each molecule is a fountain of light.
I have nothing to give my friend,
So I give you my life to amplify your might.
We are dead till we live for others.
In helping them our burden disappears.

2. Time for Reform

ABHIJIT NASKAR

6

The other day I was asked, what is a reformer? I replied, a reformer is the future happening in the present. All the possibilities that future holds, they are born in the heart of the reformer - they are born in you. Therefore, there is no time to rest, there is no time to sleep - it's time for work, it's time for sacrifice.

I say to you, I am not here to calm your nerves, I am here to set your veins on fire - your fire will give warmth to the whole world. The problem is, where you need to be calm, you burst out in rage, and where you need to be on fire, you remain indifferent. For the world to change, this behavior must change. Change your behavior and the world will change. It's that simple.

Behavior is the key to a civilized world. But what kind of behavior are we talking about! Because you see, when it comes to behavior, there is not one, but two types of behavior, one that is instinctual - the kind of behavior that helped our ancestors survive the harshness of the jungle, then there is the behavior of a civilized being - a behavior that is driven by thought and warmth - the behavior of a caring and conscientious human.

Just because we look human, doesn't mean our behavior is human - in fact, in most cases, despite calling ourselves civilized we behave the way our savage ancestors did. So, though our appearance is civilized, our behavior remains primarily the behavior of an animal living in a jungle, because that's how our instincts want us to behave, for our instincts can't tell the difference between concrete and jungle - as far as our instincts are concerned, we are still living in the jungle - hence, our primitiveness remains predominant under the guise of a civilized being.

And that's precisely what we must change. Now the question is, can we change something so intrinsic to our nature? To this I say, if primitiveness were our whole nature, then we wouldn't even be talking about a futuristic civilized world, for it would be a futile effort - but as it happens, though primitiveness is a more ancient, hence more powerful part of our nature, it is not the whole of our nature - alongside the primitiveness our brain has developed capacities, that can only be defined as humanity, with which we are to build that civilized future so many of us dream of.

Our capacities of humanity may not be as powerful as our innate primitiveness, but with each act of that humanity in our daily walks of life we make those capacities stronger, thus heading towards a future where those capacities of humanity will indeed be more powerful than our primitiveness. But this won't be easy. We will be tempted every step of the way. We will be tempted to be selfish, rather than caring - we will be tempted to be bigoted, rather than ever-growing - we will be tempted to be sectarian, rather than humanitarian - and how we behave in each of these circumstances will determine whether or not we'll succeed in building a true civilization of humans.

3. Keynote of Humanity

Great civilization demands great sacrifice. And the keynote of the human civilization – the keynote of humanity, is expansion - expansion of the self beyond the self to engulf the whole collective. One who gives up the self for the collective, will find the whole universe within the self. To put it simply, selfishness suits savages and animals, not human beings. This does not mean that you cannot engage in self-gratification once in a while - of course you can, but make sure, that you do not lose sight of the miseries of society, in your endless pursuit of self-gratification.

Self-gratification to the point of sustaining oneself is healthy, but beyond that, it's not only unhealthy, but downright inhuman. Never confuse luxury with necessity. Humble and simple, these are the watchwords of a healthy life as well as a healthy society. The lesser your needs, the stronger your integrity.

So if you want growth in life and in society, you must scale back the brakes on your desires. Focus on your purpose, not your desires. Find your role in society and carry it out with your last breath. Once you discover your purpose, every little endeavor towards that purpose will bring you joy, but if you don't have a purpose, no matter how many things you buy, it won't make you happy.

That is why I say, don't read me if you are seeking peace of mind, read me if you are dying inside for a purpose. My ideas won't give you comfort, they won't make you feel good about yourself, they won't make you calm, they will only make you restless, they'll only make you sleepless – for the world, for the society, for humanity.

Poor is not the one who has no money, poor is the one who has no purpose. But mark you, when we talk about purpose what we must keep in mind is that nobody is destined for any certain purpose, for there is no such thing as destiny. Destiny is the child of action, action is the child of realization. Once you realize your purpose in your veins, action will pour out of your veins on its own and where there is action, destiny comes running.

Veins that don't carry a purpose are no veins - nerves that don't carry ideas are no nerves. Recognize your purpose, discover the idea behind your existence and dive in with no reservation whatsoever. To hell with personal consequences, the purpose must be served – the purpose must be lived.

16

4.   The Personal Sonnet

The Personal Sonnet

If you want to be heard,
You must learn to listen.
If you want to be trusted,
You must keep trustin'.
If you want to grow,
You must first evolve.
If you want to be happy,
Let yourself dissolve.
If you want to smile,
You must learn to give.
If you want to lead,
Help others to live.
Law of the jungle is self-preservation.
Law of society is collective ascension.

5.   Politics Ain't Political

Screw politics, serve the people. I don't do politics, I do humanity. And so long as politics continue to determine the life of humanity, someone's gotta keep politics and politicians straight. And this is not just my role, this is the role of every single conscientious and accountable human being of society.

Our semi-modern democracy is founded on neither morality not merit, it's founded on popularity - as such politicians are not to be taken as some almighty overlord, beyond approach and with an olympian judgment. In fact, in a civilized society, no individual is to be aloof and inaccessible to the people.

Politicians are the conductors of society and the citizens are the musicians, only when they work together, can they produce beautiful music, otherwise, there's only noise. And just like the conductors in an orchestra, the politicians have to train themselves constantly - they must learn from the experts.

A politician who stops learning is of no use to the society. And it's these politicians that turn politics into a rotten gutter of degradation. People think when they become a politician, that's it, they no longer have to learn anything, they can do whatever they want - in fact, the reality is quite the opposite - when a person becomes an active politician the burden of learning grows ten folds, because on their learning depends the growth and security of the people. A know-it-all politician is far worse than a foolish politician.

There are two ways to look at the term politics - one is the common, predominant way, which implies politics to be a matter of the government - and this is the most savage and ill-informed interpretation of the term politics. Then there is the other way, which reveals the fundamentals of politics - and this other way is to comprehend politics the way it ought to be comprehended in a civilized society, that is, a matter of society.

Therefore, any act that involves human welfare is an act of politics - as such, science can be politics, philosophy can be politics, theology can be politics - thus, anybody who acts in the interest of human welfare is a politician, whether they hold an office or not. It is the acts that make a politician, not the office.

Everybody who acts as a responsible human being in society is a politician - this makes even me a politician, even though I do not hold office. The scientist who is responsible is a politician - the priest who is responsible is a politician - the teacher who is responsible is a politician - the janitor who is responsible is a politician - the waitress who is responsible is a politician - if you do even a single deed with the genuine intention of benefiting the society, it makes you a politician.

Every responsible human is a politician, but not every politician is a responsible human. But mark you, here the term politician is irrelevant, the only thing matters is your action with the genuine intention for good. What matters is that you are a responsible human being - what you are called is irrelevant.

6.   Removing The Whitewash

28

Society is built by determination, not designation. Even if you are called a ding-a-ling, if there is goodness in your heart, then that's what counts. You see, designation doesn't always define a person correctly. In fact, in many cases, heroes are designated as war-criminal, such as Subhas Chandra Bose, while savages are designated as heroes, such as Christopher Columbus.

And in case you are wondering who this Bose is, I'll repeat something which I have stated previously in "Hurricane Humans" - Subhas Chandra Bose is to India what George Washington is to our United States. This is the man who actually deserves the designation of "Father of India", not Gandhi. If you don't know by now, it was Subhas Chandra Bose who liberated India from British imperialism, not Gandhi, you are yet to know the history of India. Gandhi was a great scholar and thinker, but contrary to popular belief, he was not the person responsible for India's independence from British Imperialism.

Likewise, popular belief considers Christopher Columbus as some sort of hero, while in reality he was a murderer. While the world admires him as a brave explorer, all this brainless buffoon did was sail around the Caribbean and slaughtered innocent natives who greeted him with nothing but hospitality. You don't discover a land where people are already living. On top of that, when someone invades their land and starts looting, pillaging and slaughtering, he is neither brave, nor an explorer, he's just a petty thief and brut.

History is filled with such false designations, especially in favor of maintaining the illusion of white supremacy. As a matter of fact, the history of the world is a whitewashed history, where great many facts are distorted to maintain white supremacy – such as Columbus discovering America or Gandhi liberating India – Gandhi didn't liberate India, Subhas Chandra Bose did and Columbus never even set foot on America.

Thus our west is still doubtful of Bose's heroism while considering Gandhi as the face of India, because at the time when Bose was raising an army to fight against the British in India, even our United States was an ally of Britain and officially as a friend to Britain Gandhi declared that the Indians would fight in the World Wars on the side of Britain.

Gandhi had chosen the path of non-violence, which meant that he wouldn't take up arms to fight the British, even when the British continued to loot and torture the innocent natives, not unlike what Columbus did in the islands of the Caribbean. That is why, considering Gandhi as the one responsible for India's freedom is good for the image of Britain - it keeps the West as well as the East from understanding the real intensity and bloodshed that it took to liberate India from the brutal and barbaric empire of Britain. Hence, even the Rupee bills of India have the face of Gandhi.

It's like the whole world still lives in the shadow of a white, christian, straight patriarchy. The day you realize this, you'll learn all there is to learn about racism as well as sexism. Even the map of the world as we know it is one that presents a false depiction of the size of white countries. In short, it is not the map of the world that we have accepted as reality, it is a map of white supremacy.

The point is, regardless of whether our ancestors committed these mistakes of whitewashing the planet deliberately or subconsciously, we as conscientious human beings can no longer sustain these lies, we must break the spell of white-male supremacy and start living as actual civilized beings, and not as pretend civilized people, like the British imperialists and the Nazis.

Nature is never black and white, it's full of color, but you must wake up from your sleep of white supremacy to be mesmerized by those colors. To distinguish the truth from the whitewash, the spell of white supremacy must be broken. Contrary to the popular belief of ancient savages, the world doesn't revolve around white, straight, christian males - the sooner you realize this, the sooner you'll see the light of humanity.

And to do this, we must start by recognizing our errors in perception and mend those errors with actual, tangible action. For example, it's time we stop celebrating October 11 as Columbus Day and consider it as "Repentance Day", to acknowledge, and make amends for, the appalling atrocities committed by mindless and heartless oppressors like Columbus. Many have suggested that Columbus Day be replaced with Indigenous People's Day, but that would be like celebrating the assassination day of MLK as MLK day, and not his birthday.

However, to consider a single day as Repentance Day may not undo the historical wrongs committed in the name of racial, religious and cultural supremacy, but it does make way for the actual acknowledgement of those wrongs, thus making the amends more realistic and less philosophical. To right a wrong, we must first admit that a wrong has been done.

7. Conscious Corrections

Progress demands self-correction and a life of revolution. For example, shouting about gender equality once a year doesn't end the patriarchal and misogynistic stereotypes. We must live every day as women's day, only then will there be actual, practical equality in this world. We must keep the torch of equality burning every single day in our soul, and let that torch guide our action, and then only perhaps one day gender, sexuality and color will no longer be a cause for discrimination and condescension. So it all begins with our acknowledgement of the fact that misogyny is a real thing - that male chauvinism and authoritarianism are a real thing – that homophobia is a real thing – that systemic racism is a real thing.

Let me give you another example. Imagine the gall of the British Government that it continues to exhibit looted treasures from various cultures in the museum, without the slightest remorse for its inhuman exploits across the world. Any civilized people would have the common decency to return those treasures to their rightful owners, but perhaps the so-called Great Britain is yet to understand the very meaning of civilization, let alone greatness. This also explains the moronic, separatist and self-absorbed act of BREXIT.

We don't need a smaller European Union, we need a larger European Union, or a similar paradigm, that would engulf all seven continents. Here, some intellectuals may argue, we already do have the global equivalent of EU, it's called the United Nations. To them I say, United Nations is not the symbol of actually united nations of planet earth, it only pretends to be so, just like the Vatican pretends to be the authority on divinity. EU, though far from flawless, is a practical and bold manifestation of unity among several countries, whereas UN is a make belief, docile and naïve institution.

Now to get back to the matter of Brexit, you cannot expect much from a society that is yet to abolish the stone-age practice of monarchy. Here I am not referring to the entire population of the United Kingdom as stone-age, but only those Brits who actually boast about the imperialist atrocities of the British Empire - I am referring to those who are still blinded by the false and barbarian glory of their ancestors' egregious exploits across the world.

I am not saying what I am saying to enrage the common Britisher, I am saying it to make you acquainted with the inhumanities. Every nation on earth at one time or another commits acts of inhumanity, be it Britain, be it India, be it Turkey or be it our United States. The important thing is to have the grown-up guts to acknowledge them and then start working on mending those errors. We cannot undo the wrongs of our ancestors, but we can correct them by taking responsibility for them and do what's needed to make sure that we do not walk on the same path of savagery.

8.   Social and Personal Are One

Integration is imperative, but we cannot achieve that if we remain oblivious to the obstructions in integration. We must recognize those obstructions and crush them to pulp. Remember, diversity is not our weakness, it's our stronghold. The more diverse we are, the stronger we are. In this diversity lies the greatest potential for transformation. And it is an uncorrupted desire for transformation that pushes the society forward.

When the individual aims for reform in personal life, society will have all the reform it needs. In fact, if we are to make real strides in the direction of reason, unity and advancement, the very divide between social and personal must disappear from our mind. What's social must become personal, what's personal must become social. To put it simply, the person and the society can no longer stay separate - they must merge together into one indomitable force for development, without sacrificing the integrity of the environment.

Here I must mention one thing - environment and development must go hand in hand, one cannot be sacrificed for the sake of the other. We not only need integration with each other as one undivided people, but also with nature. If we don't have a place for nature in our heart, how can we expect nature to have a place for us!

Perhaps one day our very distant descendants will live on MARS, but as it has been happening with all human achievements, the rich and the privileged are the ones who would have access to those achievements first, while the rest of the world would have access years later. So, while the rich and the privileged will be living on MARS, rest of humanity on earth will be suffering because of our reckless abuse of the planet. Let me put it another – if you can't buy a Tesla you are not going to be on the nice list of the billionaire.

So, don't get overwhelmed with some billionaire's pompous dream of colonizing another planet. Unless we work diligently to dismantle the disparities of our society, no human achievement will be human achievement, for they'll only serve the benefits of the privileged, rather than serving the whole of humankind without any reservation. This is why I say, I don't have a problem with capitalism, I have a problem with capitalism without any concern for society. To some this may seem like socialism, but it's not, it's just common sense humanity.

45

9.   The Social Welfare Sonnet

The Social Welfare Sonnet

I have no problem with capitalism,
I have problem when it's devoid of society.
I have no problem with innovation,
I have problem when it lacks accountability.
I have no problem with religion,
I have problem when it's run by bigotry.
I have no problem with intellect,
I have problem when it lacks decency.
I have no problem with advancement,
I have problem when it facilitates disparity.
I have no problem with politics,
I have problem when it loses all sanity.
No field is evil entire of its own.
Evil festers when we forget we can't progress alone.

10. Conquering The Fundamental Prejudice

Service, service and service - this should be the mantra of civilized humankind, regardless of how we choose to serve - by means of innovation, by means of education, by means of justice and security or by means of a complete social reform. Whatever we do, we must do so with the welfare of people in mind - with the welfare of society in mind.

The point is, when you give up yourself to the people in need, in the end when you finally fall asleep, you'll be able to do so with your head held high. Nothing makes the head high like an act of pure selflessness for the betterment of the people. Refuse the fundamental prejudice that we ought to be selfish in order to survive - we are not, for it may suit animals, it may even suit tribal savages living in the jungle, but not modern humans of modern society.

And despite living in a modern society, if you act like a petty animal submitting to every whim of your senses, then you better start learning about humanity from scratch. Be more than a mere slave to your senses. Society still lives as slave to the senses - senses that evolved for a fierce and danger-infested life in the jungle, not for a comparatively safe environment made of concrete. Slavery of senses is the oldest form of slavery, and once we break this slavery, we'll conquer all inhumanity.

Here a particular dichotomy appears in my mind – it is that, we often see concrete as something evil, and jungle to be something beautiful, yet the fact of the matter is, jungle may appear beautiful, but that beauty holds the most vicious form of cruelty within its crevasses, whereas concrete may not appear appealing to many, yet that concrete represents the possibility of reduction in cruelty.

But the trouble is, we developed for ourselves concrete civilization much too fast for our mind to keep up with the requirements of such a society, devoid of constant threat of attacks from wild animals. So our mind does everything in its power to make sure that we pay more attention to self-preservation than anything else. The only way out of this mess is to remind ourselves, we no longer live in the jungle, hence, we cannot act like jungle animals whenever we find ourselves slipping in the direction of brutality driven by our self-serving biases.

11. **This is Not Us**
(The Sonnet)

This is Not Us
(The Sonnet)

This is not us,
Practicing savages abhorrent.
This is not sapiens,
Intelligent yet filthy indifferent.
Some think we are advanced,
But self-absorption is no advancement.
Some say we have built a free world,
But irresponsible freedom is mere derangement.
Fancy clothes and accessories make no human,
Nor do those shallow etiquettes.
When we have no kindness for others,
We are just good-looking cannibals.
This cannot be the definition of humanity.
Need of the hour is a life of inclusivity.

58

12. When Someone Does Harm

If someone harms us, then law of nature dictates that we are to retaliate by doing harm to them, but such behavior only sustains cruelty in a society. So the question that rises is, what do we do in such circumstances - do we let them do harm! And the answer is this.

When you find someone committing harm, restrain them, but don't do harm in return. Animals behave the way they do, because they can't help themselves, but humans must be better than that. It's about accountability, not some random outburst of untamed emotions.

Revolution is accountability in action, violence is selfishness in action. To put it another way, revolution is an act of accountability, violence is an act of selfishness. And service is the highest form of revolution, for service is the highest form of existence. That's why I say, I am not here to motivate you, I am here to ask you to destroy yourself (if you have not started a family of your own yet). I am here to build an army of self-sacrificing humanitarians across space and time, to march unafraid in the course of equality, inclusion and ascension, fortified with accountability, reason and acceptance.

So my question to you is - are you that army? If you are, then chisel this in your brain with the indelible ink of determination - your gospel is goodness, your religion is service, your church is society. For that soldier of mine, there is no my religion, your religion - for that soldier of mine, there is no my culture, your culture - for that soldier of mine, there is no my country, your country.

Whichever part of this earth I lay my eyes on, becomes my neighborhood. This whole world is my home and every inch of it is under my protection. You know who I am - I am a human - a human that is present in all times and ages - a human that is present beyond the reaches of ideologies, churches, monarchs and intellectuals - a human that lives beyond body and knows no bounds of sickening barriers.

13. No Throne, No Kingdom
(The Sonnet)

No Throne, No Kingdom
(The Sonnet)

I need no throne, I need no kingdom,
Human hearts are my heavenly abode.
I need no badge, I need no scepter,
Reason is my partner, warmth my zip code.
I need no praise, I need no offering,
A life of service is my paradise.
I need no reward, I need no award,
Nothing can put a price on sacrifice.
I know no etiquette, I know no manners,
These are all constructs of shallowness.
Humanity ought to drive behavior,
Humility destroys all narrowness.
To forge wholeness and sanity is our mission.
Ending all falsity let's be incarnate integration.

14. Either Expansion or Extinction

I am not left or right, but if the left seems more aligned with my ideas, it's because the left tends to be more willing to evolve, whereas the right tends to prefer its stone-age stereotypical rigidity. You see, it's not about being left or right, it's about having the capacity to recognize one's shortcomings, and having the will to correct them. Evolution is a fundamental part of life - what this means is, denial to evolve is denial of life. Expansion is the foundation of life - denial of expansion is denial of life. It's as simple as this - either expansion or extinction.

To elaborate this point further - I am not left or right, I am a human. And if someone sounds more aligned with my ideas, it doesn't necessarily mean they are left, it just means they have a more practical, community-centric and self-correcting grasp of humanity than those who are self-absorbed, self-righteous and self-serving.

This human may be known to you as Naskar, but as I said this human is present across space and time. Whenever humanity is in danger, this human will rise in one form or another - the form and the name may vary, but the purpose remains the same through eternity - the purpose to make humanity less animal and more human. And I say to you here and now, this process of becoming less animal and more human, is an endless process - it is an eternal evolution - it is an eternal expansion. And the only surefire way to do that is by recognizing and eliminating prejudices - by recognizing and eliminating stereotypes - and that too on the personal level.

15. Sonnet of Expansion

Sonnet of Expansion

I expect nothing from the world,
I have no desire to impress society.
I only care for its wellbeing,
Hence I simply do my human duty.
Don't know whether I'm left or right,
Which I don't give a damn about.
World has enough conflicts as it is,
One more duality we can do without.
Expansion is the other name of life,
Without which we are dead and rotten.
If we are not willing to evolve,
Humankind will be soon forgotten.
If today's thought is the same as yesterday,
Despite all achievements we are going astray.

16. Free Will is Not
A Question of Willpower

Stereotypes die hard, but they must, otherwise people will. But how can we eliminate stereotypes, because fact be told, you cannot actually eliminate stereotypes from your psyche, for that's the opposite of how perception works, which is, on the basis of stereotypes. One of the fundamental functions of our brain is to make assumptions about everything and everyone - to produce stereotypes - so what can you do you ask - what you can do is, recognize those stereotypes.

Let me put this into perspective. Reality is 99 percent assumption and 1 percent truth. Perception is 99 percent stereotypes and 1 percent truth (here the numbers are not to be taken literally, they are only meant to point out the stark contrast between truth and our perception of truth). Only when you are aware of this fundamental fact of life can you tread carefully in the domain of your perception.

To recognize stereotypes is to conquer them, for once you distinguish a stereotype the right, humane path appears naturally. Then comes the hard part - whether or not you choose to walk on the right path. Now here I am not talking about some philosophical or religious or theological righteousness, I am simply talking about a plain, ordinary human path, the path that is least tainted by the filthy touch of prejudice.

And whether you walk that path determines the mettle of your character. That's where the matter of free will comes in, for free will is not a question of willpower, it's a question of character. A human would rather die than compromise their character. Yet the pain-staking reality is, we have made a habit of compromising our character, with the hope of being accepted by the society.

And that is precisely what the trouble is with this whole cockeyed world of ours - it is a world where compromise of character comes easy, but practice of dignity and honor is considered impractical myth. And when people do tend to rebel, they do so not out of accountability or originality, but simply to appear cool by not conforming. Non-conformity driven by the desire to look cool is not non-conformity, it's another kind of conformity - the conformity where you give in to your own narcissistic tendencies instead of those of the society.

When the character is strong, free will takes you in a humane direction, but when the character is weak, free will takes you in the same old rotten path of primitiveness. So you see, it's all about character. Character is the foundation stone of civilization. In fact, civilization without character is not civilization, but a fancy jungle.

And once you choose the course with character over that without one, your very existence becomes a threat to every inhumanity everywhere. Then you can stand unafraid in front of the tradesmen of superstition and segregation and say out loud with utmost boldness and zero arrogance - I am injurious to prejudice, bigotry and sectarianism.

17. Simplicity is Sanity

The bold, upright spirit needs no fancy introduction, their very presence is enough to induce courage and inspiration in the hearts of others. Simplicity is the attire of those with character, sophistication is the attire of the shallow. Those who are shallow inside, look fancy outside. That's why I say to you my sibling, simplicity is priceless - simplicity is sanity - never forget that.

You won't find any fancy words in my work, because I don't know much fancy words. I think simple, I speak simple, I live simple. And what I speak of is simple, your behavior determines who you are, not your socio-cultural background. You may have read a thousand books or not, you may go to church every Sunday or not, you may pray five times a day or not, you may wear fancy suits or not, none of it matters - what matters is how you behave with the everyday, ordinary people around you.

You may be the smartest person on earth, but if you behave with others as an arrogant prick, your worth is no more than a night crawler. This is why I find it extremely liberating to act as a know-nothing simpleton wherever I am not recognized. You see, your goodness is not predicated on how intellectual you are – you don't need to be intelligent to be good - that's one of the beautiful tenets of goodness - it requires no intellect, it just requires a human heart - a heart teeming with purity and gentleness. And every heart has the capacity to be teeming with purity and gentleness, once it dismantles all egotistical nonsense that keeps that purity from manifesting.

18. **Bow O Brave**
(The Sonnet)

Bow O Brave
(The Sonnet)

Bow o brave, o lifter of hearts,
Bow in service losing all pride.
With your acts of care and community,
Make even the dust sanctified.
Selflessness and sanity,
Let these flow through your veins.
Offer up your nerves and bones,
As the world's unity lanes.
Lose all name and lose all pleasure,
Forget address to which you are born.
As you live in every person,
They will cross ocean to make you own.
Step outside the self for the unselfish has no match.
Every land will become golden by your holy touch.

19. What is Normal Human Behavior

The problem with this world is not that there is lack of goodness, the problem is, there are too many barriers to goodness. And the ludicrous part is that most of these barriers are self-imposed, which means that they exist because the individuals have consented to their existence out of their own free will, because they consider that to be normal human behavior. Let me make it absolutely clear - it's not. It is not normal human behavior to give in to barriers that divide people and to consider unity as abnormal. When you realize this, you'll know what real, normal human behavior is.

Normal human behavior is community, not self-obsession - normal human behavior is reasoning, not superstition - normal human behavior is warmth, not discrimination - normal human behavior means a plain ordinary decency towards every single human being on earth, not a suspicious condescension.

It is this simple - we cannot build a civilized world, if we do not become civilized ourselves, and everything that divides instead of unifying is uncivilized - it is inhuman. Of all the animals on earth, only the human is born with the capacity to conquer its animal nature, yet they remain oblivious to this grand, revolutionary capacity - the unparalleled capacity to influence the direction of our own evolution.

The other day I was explaining mutation to my eight year old cousin. Out of the blue she asks, can we become something else by thinking of it – in other words, can we influence mutation by thought? And this indeed is the fundamental question behind all things civilized, although I didn't expect it from an eight year old.

And the answer is, everything that we have achieved so far as an advanced species has been accomplished by thought. Every human achievement is born of thought. But mark you, thought doesn't mean thought alone, for each thought must be accompanied by action for it to bear any fruit. Thought without action is a car without wheels.

So act my friend - take a stand and act. Act with every molecule in your body. Act for not just yourself, but for the people around you. Only then can we build a caring society - only then can we build a humane society.

20. Sonnet of Breath

Sonnet of Breath

The heart holds a breath,
A breath that is indivisible.
Yet we rarely take it in,
For we are raised as vegetable.
We are seeking joy here and there,
Yet there's an ocean of it within us.
It's a joy that comes alive when we care,
At the sight of selfishness it disappears.
Intimacy breeds stability and serenity,
But not the one that thrives on body.
Intimacy that's chaste and unifying,
Manifests only in innocent amity.
Human mind is the source of all ascension.
We are the origin of all civilized creation.

96

21. Why We Suffer

The only way to build a selfless society is be selfless ourselves. I'll tell you in simple language, you live the best life when you live for others. We suffer because our brain doesn't know that we are living in a modern society - it still believes that we are living in the jungle, hence it does everything in its power to keep us on our toes all the time, by means of fear, insecurity, anxiety and a whole lot of illusive suffering. Behind all of this, there is only one simple drive that's at play - the drive for self-preservation - the drive for survival of the self - in short, it's all a subconscious manifestation of selfishness - selfishness at its most raw.

We suffer because we are selfish, whether we know it or not. And we cannot eliminate that suffering by resisting it, but we can make it powerless - we can make it obsolete - how you ask - simple - forget what's gonna happen to you in the future. To hell with the self and for others be the help. Their smile, their joy, their contentment will fill your heart with inexplicable bliss, which can never be achieved with self-centricity. The antidote to suffering is life and the seed of life is service.

Without an uncorrupted, unbending and upright sense of service from a handful of headstrong and heartstrong individuals, no God can lift the human society. God is the placebo for the masses, it may solve trivial problems of society, but to treat the big issues, what is required is actual medicine, that is, actual, tangible human intervention. That is why I don't worship Gods, I make them.

The realization of humanity comes not to the selfish snobs, but only to selfless Gods - Gods who have given up the self - Gods who know no other life but to live for others. Salvation is theirs to command, progress is theirs to command, civilization is theirs to command. So, don't wait and pray my friend, go out there and build the world. Live your life as a sacrifice to remember, and humankind is bound to flourish.

22. Human Helpline
(The Sonnet)

Human Helpline
(The Sonnet)

Neither Christ, nor Krishna, nor Superman,
No imagination can rescue humanity.
Each of us is the only helpline,
Human salvation is human responsibility.
Enough with these prayer and rituals,
Now awake from the sleep of subjugation.
As heroes fraught with reason and conscience,
We must rise to break all submission.
Progress demands a life of revolution,
Self-induced slavery won't do.
The more you seek a savior outside,
The more you turn into boneless goo.
Of all life on earth the human being is peerless.
Only those called sapiens roar for the helpless.

23. Practical Divinity

However, many people do still need their god, and to them I say, if you need a god, keep it - everybody has imaginary friends, my imaginary friend is my late teacher, and I find it therapeutic to talk to him whenever I hit rock bottom. But what does it have to do with religion - it's just something we humans need to survive, quite like water and food! The last thing this world needs is more war to prove whose imaginary friend is better than the rest. And above all, never use god as an excuse for your inaction or your prejudices.

Divinity needs no god, for divinity lies in your sense of community. Worldliness is shallowness, community is wholeness. As I've said in one of my previous works, one who feels responsible for their community, needs to ancestral identity. Your identity is in your responsibility towards the people. Laziness won't do, recklessness won't do - call upon the endless streams of courage within your veins and come aboard the vessel of civilization to work with tremendous energy for those who have lost all hope.

There are too many people working to better the lives of those who already have more than they need, yet those who are in need of real help spend each day with no hope or help to speak of - why my friend - why - they are waiting for you - they are wailing for you - don't you hear them - don't you hear their tears dropping on the lifeless soil beneath their feet! You worry about philosophical questions like, if a tree falls in a forest and nobody is there to hear it, does it make a sound - yet you pay no attention to real questions of life and death that actually require your intervention more than any philosophical question in the world! Why - I ask you again - why - why is it that philosophy, technology and argumentation have more grip over your psyche than the actual troubles of the people! Don't answer me - just think - think and when you have thought enough, shred all shallow philosophical pomp and rush right away to the helpless, the forgotten, the destitute as the real, practical answer to their life.

Remember this, sooner or later in our life, each of us is called upon to improve the conditions of others - and when we are, we must rise to the occasion and become world-builders. We must rise to the occasion as reformers - the kind that history has never seen before.

24. Adopt A Neighborhood
(The Sonnet)

Adopt A Neighborhood
(The Sonnet)

Adopt a neighborhood,
Make their problems your own.
This is the only road to life,
Society's hope is you alone.
Charity, security and world peace,
All these are cosmetic theory.
When you learn to live as human,
You'll see their actual foolery.
When our voices combine,
All noise turns melody of heavens.
Joy is amplified a hundred times,
We lose sense of all our burdens.
Diversity and progress will come alright,
Once you perceive beyond your selfish sight.

25. No Time for Argumentation

I don't have time for mystical nonsense, I don't have time for intellectual argumentation - real problems of the world keep me busy enough. No mysticism has ever solved any problem of society, it only provides comfort to some tired and sleepy souls, it makes them feel good about their absolute nonchalance towards the troubles of society that continue to put humans in harm's way. You see, real problems require real solutions - they require you - your mind, your body, your entire being as a living, breathing human.

The lower the animal, the more selfish it is - higher animals are selfless animals, they are the real humans. Mysticism is an act of selfishness, argumentation is an act of selfishness, discrimination is an act of selfishness, bigotry is an act of selfishness - in short, all these traits are the archetypes of animal behavior, not human.

Many philosophers argue that intellect makes us superior to the rest of the animals on earth. I say, intellect doesn't make us higher or lower, selflessness does. Selfish intellect may turn a species into the masters of a planet overnight (metaphorically speaking), but it can't sustain the serenity and sanity of that species in the long run. A species that lives by intellect, dies by intellect. It's only with selflessness can we sustain a species.

It is this simple, absence of self in the individual means presence of the self in everyone. The torch of progress burns bright and long spreading light only if it is held by selfless hands - in the hands of the selfish it burns bright for a brief period then goes out all of a sudden while burning everything to ashes.

And when the torch of progress is held by selfless hands, we no longer need to pay special attention to matters of integration and assimilation - you know why - because selflessness destroys all division amongst humankind. Let me put it in even simpler terms, you are dead till you live for others.

26. The Final Solution
(A Sonnet)

The Final Solution
(A Sonnet)

O new people, o new humanizers,
The world has been waiting for you long.
Waiting for your dawn with deepest zeal,
Society is weary yet tries to be strong.
Now rise o makers of civilization,
Replenish this death valley with your sanctity.
Make rigidity and prejudice quiver,
Sanitize humanity with rapids of indivisibility.
The sun has gone dark, the moon lost its glory,
All are waiting for your galvanizing advent.
These deserts can no more sustain life,
You alone are hope and the last encouragement.
Walk boldly as the awakening of revolution.
Wake up from indifference and be the final solution.

27. Not Woke, Just Human

The problem is, most people either care too much about what society thinks of them, or not at all - and very few actually care for the welfare of society. And that's precisely the kind of humans this world needs - in fact, that's the only people who deserve the title human, rest as I mentioned earlier, are mere animals.

Care for the welfare of society, not their opinion of you - to hell with what they think of you, just do your best for the elevation of others - not as a leader, but as a servant - not as a know-it-all nimrod, but as a self-correcting sage - seek no reward, seek no applause, just keep on walking in the course of your cause.

Don't compromise your cause to adjust with society, persist on your cause and the society will correct itself to adjust to you. And in the process, avoid pledging allegiance to any and all lobbies, be it the woke lobby or the neoliberal lobby or the conservative lobby or any other. Allegiance to ideology shrinks your original humanity, regardless of whether it's called being woke or being proud.

Woke and cancel culture are both signs of a judgmental culture, not a mentally mature one.

These are murky waters, so please go very slow. A world where you cannot even speak to another person without worrying about what they are going to think of you, has not advanced much from the days when the white people used to own slaves. Let me tell you this, if you are kind, if you are compassionate, if you hold no discrimination towards people whatsoever, then you have no reason to worry about whether you are woke enough. As I said, stand strong as a decent human being, and the whole society will make adjustments to adapt to you.

A being of reason and warmth is the standard of measure for all labels, not the other way around. For example, the moment you call me woke, is the moment you deny me altogether – the moment you call me liberal, is the moment you deny me altogether – the moment you call me socialist, is the moment you deny me altogether. On a cursory study of my work, they may seem like appropriate titles to depict it, but no theoretical title can successfully depict a whole human being.

However, different people have different ways of dealing with life. As my teacher used to say and still says in my head, plenty are the tastes, so are the paths. So, do not look down on them just because their path differs from yours - remember, as long a person's chosen path does not involve discrimination and bigotry, they are as much a rightful part of the human society as you and I. No path is perfect, no human is perfect. We all have our shortcomings, just like we all have our own unique strengths - so why not acknowledge and embrace those strengths of each other and make up for each other's shortcomings! Life is too precious to be wasted on petty squabbles.

Be a human and stand by those who practice humanity, without paying any attention to which path or lobby they adhere to. Every generation has their own way of dealing with the world, hence they come up with new terms for same old human behaviors. What used to be called censorship, is now called cancel culture - what used to be called freethought, is now called woke culture. And of course, these acts of defining old concepts with new terms is somewhat intrinsic to the human species, but you must remain cautious never to let these terminologies take over your plain ordinary sense of humanity.

Leave the labeling for the political analysts and pompous intellectuals, we are revolutionaries - we are here to build civilization with our blood and sweat, not to argue on philosophies over a cup of coffee.

You want to fly, I say break your chains first. The best path is to have no path. The path of emptiness is the path of wholeness. One who is empty of all labels, contains the whole humanity in their chest. Be the example of a whole and indivisible humankind, not a divided and puny one. Remind yourself - I am not woke, I am just human - I am not socialist, I am just human - I am not wise, I am just human. Stand up, look ahead, jaw firm, spine upright, and say out loud - I am the essence of determination - I am speculation, aspiration, the spirit of ascension - I am the peace call of evolution - I am togetherness itself sisters and brothers - I am life, I am breath, I am humanite, a human dynamite that destroys every inhumanity that crosses its path.

Humanity is the highest form of love there is, and love needs no lobby, label or ideology, for love itself is everything that is human about us - we are either living in it, enveloped in its wholeness or we are analyzing it with intellect from outside while dying for a taste of it.

Integration is an act of love, not intellect. A person may be an intellectual yet be a savage, but a person of love can never be a savage, for love and savagery are antithesis of each other. A person of ritual is respected in their own circle, a person of intellect is respected in some circles, a person of love is respected everywhere. Everything be sacrificed for love, love be sacrificed for nothing. Love is the highest truth, all else are lesser replicas.

But this love is not the love of expectation - it is not the love of flesh - it is not the love of the senses - this love is timeless, it is devoid of expectation, it is chaste, pure and absolutely untainted by intellectual disguise as well as rigid brutality of society. Only with such love, pure and undying can we lift this world up in our heart and watch it flourish and shine through the fabric of time.

BIBLIOGRAPHY

Archer M., (2000), Being Human: The Problem of Agency. Cambridge University Press.

Archer M., (2003), Structure, Agency and the Internal Conversation. Cambridge University Press.

Adolphs R (2003) Cognitive neuroscience of human social behaviour. Nature Rev Neurosci 4: 165–178.

Adolphs R, Tranel D, Damasio AR (2003) Dissociable neural systems for recognizing emotions. Brain Cogn 52: 61–69.

Afton, A. D. (1985). Forced copulation as a reproductive strategy of male lesser scaup: A field test of some predictions. - Behaviour 92, p. 146-167.

Allison T, Puce A, McCarthy G. (2000) Social perception from visual cues: role of the STS region. Trends Cogn Sci 4: 267–278.

Andresen, Jensine, and Robert Forman, eds. Cognitive Models and Spiritual Maps. Bowling Green, Ohio: Imprint Academic, 2000.

Ashbrook, James, and Carol Albright. The Humanizing Brain: Where Religion and Neuroscience Meet. Cleveland, OH: Pilgrim Press, 1997.

Azari, Nina, Janpeter Nickel, Gilbert Wunderlich, Michael Niedeggen, Harald Hefter, Lutz Tellmann, Hans Herzog, Petra Stoerig, Dieter Birnbacher, and Rudiger Seitz. "Neural Correlates of Religious Experience." European Journal of Neuroscience 13, no. 8 (2001)

Agar, N. (2004). Liberal eugenics: In defence of human enhancement. London: Blackwell Publishing.

Alteheld, N., Roessler, G., Vobig, M., & Walter, R. (2004). The retina implant new approach to a visual prosthesis. Biomedizinische Technik, 49(4), 99–103.

Antal, A., Nitsche, M. A., Kincses, T. Z., Kruse, W., Hoffmann, K. P., & Paulus, W. (2004a). Facilitation of visuo-motor learning by transcranial direct current stimulation of the motor and extrastriate visual areas in humans. European Journal of Neuroscience, 19(10), 2888–2892.

Bhat Z, Kumar, S, Bhat H (2015) In vitro meat production. Challenges and benefits over conventional meat production. J Sci Food Agric 14: 241–248

Bernstein R. J., (1967), John Dewey. New York: Washington Square Press.

Bernstein R.J., (1971), Praxis and Action: Contemporary Philosophies of Human Activity. Philadelphia: University of Pennsylvania Press.

Bernstein R.J., (1976), The Restructuring Social and Political Thought.

Bernstein R.J., (1983), Beyond Relativism and Objectivism: Science, Hermeneutics, and Praxis. Philadelphia: University of Pennsylvania Press.

Bernstein R.J., (1986), Philosophical Profiles. Philadelphia: University of Pennsylvania Press.

Bernstein R.J., (1991), New Constellation. Cambridge: MIT Press.

Barash, D. P. (1977). Sociobiology of rape in mallards (Anas platyrhynchos): Responses of the mated male. - Science 197, p. 788-789.

Berger, J. (1986). Wild horses of the great basin: Social competition and population size. - The University of Chicago Press, Chicago.

Birkhead, T. R., Johnson, S. D. & Nettleship, D. N. (1985). Extra-pair matings and mate guarding in the common murre Uria aalge. - Anim. Behav. 33, p. 608-619.

Beauregard, Mario, and Vincent Paquette. "Neural Correlates of a Mystical Experience in Carmelite Nuns." Neuroscience Letters 405, no. 3 (2006)

Benson, Herbert. Timeless Healing: The Power and Biology of Belief. New York: Scribner, 1996

Bogen, J.E.(1995a), 'On the neurophysiology of consciousness: Part I. An overview', Consciousness and Cognition, 4.

Bogen, J.E. (1995b), 'On the neurophysiology of consciousness: Part II. Constraining the semantic problem', Consciousness and Cognition, 4.

Bremner, J. D., R. Soufer, et al. (2001). "Gender differences in cognitive and neural correlates of remembrance of emotional words." Psychopharmacol Bull 35 (3).

Brothers, L. (2002). The social brain: A project for integrating primate behavior and neurophysiology in a new domain. In J. T. Cacioppo et al. (Eds.), Foundations in neuroscience. Cambridge, MA: MIT Press.

Buss, D. D. (2003). Evolutionary Psychology: The New Science of Mind, 2nd ed. New York: Allyn & Bacon.

Buss, D. M. (1989). "Conflict between the sexes: Strategic interference and the evocation of anger and upset." J Pers Soc Psychol 56 (5).

Buss, D. M. (1995). "Psychological sex differences. Origins through sexual selection." Am Psychol 50 (3).

Buss, D. M. (2002). "Review: Human Mate Guarding." Neuro Endocrinol Lett 23 (Suppl 4).

Buss, D. M., and D. P. Schmitt (1993). "Sexual strategies theory: An evolutionary perspective on human mating." Psychol Rev 100 (2).

Blakemore SJ, Decety J (2001) From the perception of action to the understanding of intention. Nature Rev Neurosci 2: 561.

Bruce C, Desimone R, Gross CG (1981) Visual properties of neurons in a polysensory area in superior temporal sulcus of the macaque. J Neurophysiol 46: 369–384.

Buccino G, Vogt S, Ritzl A, Fink GR, Zilles K, Freund HJ, Rizzolatti G (2004) Neural circuits underlying imitation of hand actions: an event related fMRI study. Neuron 42: 323–34.

Colapietro V., (1988), "Human Agency: The Habits of Our Being."

Southern Journal of Philosophy, XXVI, 2, pp. 153-68.

Colapietro V., (1992), "Purpose, Power, and Agency." The Monist, 75, 4 (October) pp. 423-44.

Colapietro V., (2003), "Signs and their vicissitudes: Meanings in excess of consciousness and functionality." Logica, Dialogica, Ideologica, a cure di Susan Petrilli e Patrizia Calefato (Milano: Mimesis), pp. 221-36.

Colapietro V., (2004a), "C. S. Peirce's Reclamation of Teleology." Nature in American Philosophy, ed. Jean De Groot (Washington, D.C.: Catholic University Press of America), pp. 88-108.

Colapietro V., (2004b), "Portrait of a Historicist: An Alternative Reading of Peircean Semiotic." Semiotiche, 2/04 [maggio 2004], pp. 49-68.

Colapietro V., (2006), "Engaged Pluralism: Between Alterity and

Sociality." The Pragmatic Century: Conversations with Richard J. Bernstein (Albany, NY: SUNY Press), pp. 39-68.

Colapietro V., (2009), "Habit, Competence, and Purpose." Forthcoming in The Transactions of the Charles S. Peirce Society. Calder AJ, Keane J, Manes F, Antoun N, Young AW (2000) Impaired recognition and experience of disgust following brain injury. Nature Neurosci 3: 1077–1078.

Carey DP, Perrett DI, Oram MW (1997) Recognizing, understanding and reproducing actions. In: Jeannerod M, Grafman J (eds) Handbook of neuropsychology. Vol. 11: Action and cognition. Elsevier, Amsterdam.

Carr L, Iacoboni M, Dubeau MC, Mazziotta JC, Lenzi GL (2003) Neural mechanisms of empathy in humans: a relay from neural systems for imitation to limbic areas. Proc Natl Acad Sci USA 100: 5497–5502.

Changeux JP, Ricoeur P (1998) La nature et la règle. Odile Jacob, Paris.

Cochin S, Barthelemy C, Roux S, Martineau J (1999) Observation and execution of movement: similarities demonstrated by quantified electroencephalograpy. Eur J Neurosci 11: 1839– 1842.

Chomsky Noam, (2017) Requiem for the American Dream

Chomsky Noam, (2016) Who Rules the World?

Chomsky Noam, (2010) How the World Works

Churchland, P.S. (1986), Neurophilosophy (Cambridge, MA: The MIT Press).

Churchland, P.S. & Ramachandran, V.S. (1993), 'Filling in: Why Dennett is wrong', in Dennett and His Critics:

Demystifying Mind, ed. B. Dahlbom (Oxford: Blackwell Scientific Press).

Churchland, P.S., Ramachandran, V.S. & Sejnowski, T.J. (1994), 'A critique of pure vision', in Large- scale Neuronal Theories of the Brain, ed. C. Koch & J.L. Davis (Cambridge, MA: The MIT Press).

Crick, F. (1994), The Astonishing Hypothesis: The Scientific Search for the Soul (New York: Simon and Schuster).

Crick, F. (1996), 'Visual perception: rivalry and consciousness', Nature, 379.

Crick, F. & Koch, C. (1992), 'The problem of consciousness', Scientific American, 267.

Craig AD (2002) How do you feel? Interoception: the sense of the physiological condition of the body. Nature Rev Neurosci 3: 655–666.

Damasio, A (2003a) Looking for Spinoza. Harcourt Inc. Damasio A (2003b) Feeling of emotion and the self. Ann NY Acad Sci 1001: 253–261.

d'Aquili, Eugene. "Senses of Reality in Science and Religion." Zygon 17, no 4 (1982)

d'Aquili, Eugene. "The Biopsychological Determinants of Religious Ritual Behavior." Zygon 10, no. 1 (1975)

d'Aquili, Eugene. "The Myth-Ritual Complex: A Biogenetic Structural Analysis." Zygon 18, no. 3 (1983)

d'Aquili, Eugene, and Andrew Newberg. The Mystical Mind: Probing the Biology of Religious Experience. Minneapolis: Fortress Press, 1999.

Daly DD. 1958. Ictal affect. Am J Psychiatry.

Damasio, A. (1994) Descartes' Error: Emotion, Reason and the Human Brain. New York, Putnams.

Damasio, A. (1999) The Feeling of What Happens: Body, Emotion and the Making of Consciousness. London, Heinemann.

Darwin, C. (1859) On the Origin of Species by Means of Natural Selection. London, Murray.

Darwin, C. (1871) The Descent of Man and Selection in Relation to Sex. London, John Murray.

Darwin, C. (1872) The Expression of the Emotions in Man and Animals. London, John Murray; also published 1965, Chicago, University of Chicago Press.

Dawkins, M.S. (1987) Minding and mattering. In C. Blakemore and S. Greenfield (eds) Mindwaves. Oxford, Blackwell, 151-60.

Dawkins, R. (1976) The Selfish Gene. Oxford, Oxford University Press; a new edition, with additional material, was published in 1989.

Dawkins, R. (1986) The Blind Watchmaker. London, Longman.

Di Pellegrino G, Fadiga L, Fogassi L, Gallese V, Rizzolatti G (1992) Understanding motor events: A neurophysiological study. Exp Brain Res 91: 176–80.

Deikman, A.J. (2000) A functional approach to mysticism. Journal of Consciousness Studies 7(11-12), 75-91.

Delmonte, M.M. (1987) Personality and meditation. In M. West (ed.) The Psychology of Meditation. Oxford, Clarendon Press, 118-32.

Dennett, D.C. (1987) The Intentional Stance. Cambridge, MA, MIT Press.

Dennett, D.C. (1988) Quining qualia. In A.J. Marcel and E. Bisiach (eds)

Consciousness in Contemporary Science. Oxford, Oxford University Press, 42-77.

Dennett, D.C. (1991) Consciousness Explained. Boston, MA, and London, Little, Brown and Co.

Dennett, D.C. (1995a) Darwin's Dangerous Idea. London, Penguin.

Dennett, D.C. (1995b) The unimagined preposterousness of zombies. Journal of Consciousness Studies 2(4), 322-6.

Dennett, D.C. (1995c) Cog: steps towards consciousness in robots. In T. Metzinger (ed.) Conscious Experience. Thorverton, Devon, Imprint Academic, 471-87.

Dennett, D.C. (1995d) The path not taken. Behavioral and Brain Sciences 18, 252-3; commentary on N. Block, On a confusion about a function of consciousness. Behavioral and Brain Sciences 18, 227.

Dennett, D.C. (1996a) Facing backwards on the problem of consciousness. Journal of Consciousness Studies 3(1), 4-6.

Dennett, D.C. (1996b) Kinds of Minds: Towards an Understanding of Consciousness. London, Weidenfeld & Nicolson.

Dennett, D.C. (1997) An exchange with Daniel Dennett. In J. Searle (ed.) The Mystery of Consciousness. New York, New York Review of Books, 115-19.

Dennett, D.C. (1998) The myth of double transduction. In S.R. Hameroff, A.W. Kaszniak and A. C. Scott (eds) Toward a Science of Consciousness: The Second Tucson Discussions and Debates. Cambridge, MA, MIT Press, 97-107.

Dennett, D.C. (1998b) Brainchildren: Essays on Designing Minds. Cambridge, MA, MIT Press.

Dennett, D.C. (2001) The fantasy of first person science. Debate with D. Chalmers, Northwestern University, Evanston, IL, February 2001.

Dennett, D.C. (2003) Freedom Evolves. New York, Penguin.

Dennett, D.C. and Kinsbourne, M. (1992) Time and the observer: the where and when of consciousness in the brain. Behavioral and Brain Sciences 15, 183-247, including commentaries and authors' responses.

Dewey J., (1911 [1977]), "Epistemological Realism: The Alleged Ubiquity of the Knowledge Relation." Journal of Philosophy, VIII, 20 (September 28, 1911).

Dewhurst, Kenneth, and A. W. Beard. "Sudden Religious Conversions in Temporal Lobe Epilepsy." British Journal of Psychiatry 117 (1970)

Dewhurst K, Beard AW. Sudden religious conversions in temporal lobe epilepsy. 1970 Epilepsy Behav 2003

Devinsky O, Lai G. Spirituality and religion in epilepsy. Epilepsy Behav 2008.

Devinsky, O., Morrell, MJ, Vogt, BA. (1995) 'Contribution of anterior cingulate cortex to behavior', Brain, 118.

Douglas Stone A., Chapter 24, The Indian Comet, in the book Einstein and the Quantum, Princeton University Press, Princeton, New Jersey, 2013.

E. Horvitz, "One Hundred Year Study on Artificial Intelligence: Reflections and Framing," ed: Stanford University, 2014.

Einstein A. (1925). "Quantentheorie des einatomigen idealen Gases". Sitzungsberichte der Preussischen Akademie der Wissenschaften.

Eckhart Meister, Selected Writings

Egidi R., ed. (1999), "Von Wright and 'Dante's Dream': Stages in a Philosophical Pilgrim's Progress", in In Search of a New Humanism: the Philosophy of G.H. von Wright, ed. by R. Egidi, Kluwer, Dordrecht.

Fadiga L, Fogassi L, Pavesi G, Rizzolatti G (1995) Motor facilitation during action observation: a magnetic stimulation study. J Neurophysiol 73: 2608–2611.

Fogassi L, Gallese V, Fadiga L, Rizzolatti G (1998) Neurons responding to the sight of goal directed hand/arm actions in the parietal area PF (7b) of the macaque monkey. Soc Neurosci Abs 24:257.5.

Frith U, Frith CD (2003) Development and neurophysiology of mentalizing. Philos Trans R Soc Lond B Biol Sci 358: 459.

Farah, M.J. (1989), 'The neural basis of mental imagery', Trends in Neurosciences, 10.

Finlay BL, Darlington RB (1995) Linked regularities in the development and evolution of mammalian brains. Science 268.

Freud, S. "The Interpretation of Dreams", 1900

Freud, S. "Selected papers on hysteria and other psychoneuroses" Journal of Nervous and Mental Disease 1909.

Freud, S. "The Origin and Development of Psychoanalysis", 1910

Freud, S. "Psychopathology of everyday life", 1914

Freud, S. "Beyond the Pleasure Principle", 1920

Frith, C.D. & Dolan, R.J. (1997), 'Abnormal beliefs: Delusions and memory', Paper presented at the May,

1997, Harvard Conference on Memory and Belief.

Gay, Volney, ed. Neuroscience and Religion. Plymouth, UK: Lexington Books, 2009.

Gazzaniga, M. S. (1985). The social brain. New York: Basic Books.

Gazzaniga, M.S. (1993), 'Brain mechanisms and conscious experience', Ciba Foundation Symposium, 174.

Geschwind N. "Behavioural changes in temporal lobe epilepsy". Psychol Med. 1979.

Gellhorn, E., Kiely, W.F. "Mystical states of consciousness: neurophysiological and clinical aspects." J Nerv Ment Dis. 1972;154:399-405.

Gilbert SL, Dobyns WB, Lahn BT (2005) Genetic links between brain development and brain evolution. Nat Rev Genet 6.

Gray JA. The Psychology of Fear and Stress. 2nd ed. New York, NY: Cambridge University Press; 1988.

Gloor, P. (1992), 'Amygdala and temporal lobe epilepsy', in The Amygdala: Neurobiological Aspects of Emotion, Memory and Mental Dysfunction, ed J.P. Aggleton (New York: Wiley-Liss).

Greenspan, S. I. and S. G. Shanker (2004). The first idea: How symbols, language, and intelligence evolved from our early primate ancestors to modern humans. Cambridge, MA: Da Capo Press.

Grady, D. (1993), 'The vision thing: Mainly in the brain', Discover, June.

Gallagher HL, Frith CD (2003) Functional imaging of 'theory of mind'. Trends Cogn Sci 7: 77.

Gallese V, Fogassi L, Fadiga L, Rizzolatti G (2002) Action representation and the inferior parietal lobule. In: Prinz W, Hommel B (eds) Attention & Performance XIX. Common mechanisms in perception and action. Oxford University Press, Oxford.

Gallese V, Keysers C, Rizzolatti G (2004) A unifying view of the basis of social cognition. Trends Cogn Sci 8: 396–403.

Gangitano M, Mottaghy FM, Pascual-Leone A (2001) Phase specific modulation of cortical motor output during movement observation. NeuroReport 12: 1489–1492.

Gangitano M, Mottaghy FM, Pascual-Leone A (2004) Modulation of premotor mirror neuron activity during observation of unpredictable grasping movements. Eur J Neurosci 20: 2193– 2202.

Goldman AI, Sripada CS (2004) Simulationist models of face-based emotion recognition. Cognition 94: 193–213.

Grèzes J, Costes N, Decety J (1998) Top-down effect of strategy on the perception of human biological motion: a PET investigation. Cogn Neuropsychol 15: 553–582.

Grèzes J, Armony JL, Rowe J, Passingham RE (2003) Activations related to "mirror" and "canonical" neurones in the human brain: an fMRI study. Neuroimage 18: 928–937.

Gross CG, Rocha-Miranda CE, Bender DB (1972) Visual properties of neurons in the inferotemporal cortex of the macaque. J Neurophysiol 35: 96–111.

Hari R, Forss N, Avikainen S, Kirveskari S, Salenius S, Rizzolatti G (1998) Activation of human primary motor cortex during action observation: a neuromagnetic study.

Proc. Natl Acad Sci USA 95: 15061–15065.

Hardy, G. H. (1940). Ramanujan. Cambridge: Cambridge University Press.

Hall, Daniel, Keith Meador, and Harold Koenig. "Measuring Religiousness in Health Research: Review and Critique." Journal of Religion and Health 47, no. 2 (2008)

Harris, Sam, Jonas Kaplan, Ashley Curiel, Susan Bookheimer, Marco Iacoboni, and Mark Cohen. "The Neural Correlates of Religious and Nonreligious Belief." PLoS One 4, no. 10 (October 1, 2009)

Halgren, E. (1992), 'Emotional neurophysiology of the amygdala within the context of human cognition', in The Amygdala: Neurobiological Aspects of Emotion, Memory and Mental Dysfunction, ed J.P. Aggleton (New York: Wiley-Liss).

Halligan PW, Fink GR, Marshal JC, Vallar G. 2003. Spatial cognition: evidence from visual neglect. Trends Cogn Sci.

Handbook of Emotions, Edited by Michael Lewis, Jeannette M. Haviland-Jones, and Lisa Feldman Barrett, The Guilford Press; 3rd edition (2010).

Haggard, P., Clark, S. and Kalogeras,]. (2002) Voluntary action and conscious awareness, Nature Neuroscience 5, 382-5. Haggard, P., Newman, C. and Magno, E. (1999) On the perceived time of voluntary actions. British Journal of Psychology 90, 291-303.

Hameroff, S.R. and Penrose, R. (1996) Conscious events as orchestrated space-time selections. Journal of Consciousness Studies 3(1), 36-53; also reprinted in J. Shear (ed.) (1997) Explaining Consciousness-The Hard Problem. Cambridge, MA, MIT Press, 177-95.

Hardcastle, V.G. (2000) How to understand theN in NCC. InT. Metzinger (ed.) Neural Correlates of Consciousness. Cambridge, MA, MIT Press, 259-64.

Harding, D.E. (1961) On Having no Head: Zen and the Re-Discovery of the Obvious. London, Buddhist Society.

Hardy, A. (1979) The Spiritual Nature of Man: A Study of Contemporary Religious Experience. Oxford, Clarendon Press.

Hamad, S. (1990) The symbol grounding problem. Physica D 42, 335-46.

Hamad, S. (2001) No easy way out. The Sciences 41(2), 36-42.

Harre, R. and Gillett, G. (1994) The Discursive Mind. Thousand Oaks, CA, Sage.

Haugeland, J. (ed.) (1997) Mind Design II: Philosophy, Psychology, Artificial

Intelligence. Cambridge, MA, MIT Press.

Hauser, M.D. (2000) Wild Minds: What Animals Really Think. New York, Henry Holt and Co.; London, Penguin.

Hearne, K. (1990) The Dream Machine. Northants, Aquarian.

Hebb, D.O. (1949) The Organization of Behavior. New York, Wiley.

Helmholtz, H.L.F. von (1856-67) Treatise on Physiological Optics.

Hess, EH (1975) "The role of pupil size in communication," Scientific American, 233(5), 110–12.

Heyes, C.M. (1998) Theory of mind in nonhuman primates. Behavioral and Brain Sciences 21, 101-48; with commentaries.

Heyes, C.M. and Galef, B.G. (eds) (1996) Social Learning in Animals: The Roots of Culture. San Diego, CA, Academic Press.

Hilgard, E.R. (1986) Divided Consciousness: Multiple Controls in Human Thought and Action. New York, Wiley.

Hocquette JF (2016) Is in vitro meat the solution for the future? Meat Science 120: 167–176

Hodgson, R. (1891) A case of double consciousness. Proceedings of the Society for Psychical Research 7, 221-58.

Hofstadter, D.R. (1979) Code!, Escher, Bach: An Eternal Golden Braid. London, Penguin.

Hofstadter, D.R. and Dennett, D.C. (eds) (1981) The Mind's I: Fantasies and Reflections on Self and Soul. London, Penguin.

Holland, J. (ed.) (2001) Ecstasy: The Complete Guide: A Comprehensive Look at the Risks and Benefits of MDMA. Rochester, VT, Park Street Press.

Holmes, D.S. (1987) The influence of meditation versus rest on physiological arousal. In M. West (ed.) The Psychology of Meditation. Oxford, Clarendon Press, 81-103.

Holmstrom, David. 1992, Christian Science Monitor

Holt, J. (1999) Blindsight in debates about qualia. Journal of Consciousness Studies 6(5), 54-71.

Horgan, J. (1994), 'Can science explain consciousness?', Scientific American, 271.

Holloway RL (1996) Evolution of the human brain. In: Lock A, Peters CR (eds) Handbook of human symbolic evolution. Oxford University Press, Oxford

Iacoboni M, Woods RP, Brass M, Bekkering H, Mazziotta JC, Rizzolatti G (1999) Cortical mechanisms of human imitation. Science 286: 2526–2528.

Iacoboni M, Koski LM, Brass M, Bekkering H, Woods RP, Dubeau MC, Mazziotta JC, Rizzolatti G (2001) Reafferent copies of imitated actions in the right superior temporal cortex. Proc Natl Acad Sci USA 98: 13995–13999.

Jeannerod M (1988) The neural and behavioural organization of goal-directed movements. Clarendon Press, Oxford.

Johnson-Frey SH, Maloof FR, Newman-Norlund R, Farrer C, Inati S, Grafton ST (2003) Actions or hand-objects interactions? Human inferior frontal cortex and action observation. Neuron 39: 1053–1058.

Jackson, F. (1982) Epiphenomenal qualia. Philosophical Quarterly 32, 127-36.

James, W. (1890) The Principles of Psychology (2 volumes). London, Macmillan.

James, W. (1902) The Varieties of Religious Experience: A Study in Human Nature. New York and London, Longmans, Green and Co.

Jansen, K. (2001) Ketamine: Dreams and Realities. Sarasota, FL, Multidisciplinary Association for Psychedelic Studies.

Jay, M. (ed.) (1999) Artificial Paradises: A Drugs Reader. London, Penguin.

Jaynes, J. (1976) The Origin of Consciousness in the Breakdown of the Bicameral Mind. New York, Houghton Mifflin.

Johnson, M.K. and Raye, C.L. (1981) Reality monitoring. Psychological Review 88, 67-85.

Kadim I, Mahgoub O, Baqir S et al. (2015) Cultured meat from muscle stem cells: a review of challenges and prospects. J Integr Agr 14: 222–233

Koski L, Iacoboni M, Dubeau MC, Woods RP, Mazziotta JC (2003) Modulation of cortical activity during different imitative behaviors. J Neurophysiol 89: 460–471.

Krolak-Salmon P, Henaff MA, Isnard J, Tallon-Baudry C, Guenot M, Vighetto A, Bertrand O, Mauguiere F (2003) An attention modulated response to disgust in human ventral anterior insula. Ann Neurol 53: 446–453.

Kandel, E. R. In Search of Memory: The Emergence of a New Science of Mind, W. W. Norton & Company (2007).

Kandel E. R. Schwartz JH, Jessel TM. Principles of neural sciences. New York; McGraw Hill, 2000.

Kanizsa, G. (1979), Organization In Vision (New York: Praeger).

Kaloupek DG, Scott JR, Khatami V. Assessment of coping strategies associated with syncope in blood donors. J Psychosom Res. 1985;29:207-214.

Kanwisher, N. (2001) Neural events and perceptual awareness. Cognition 79, 89-113; also reprinted inS. Dehaene (ed.) The Cognitive Neuroscience of Consciousness. Cambridge, MA, MIT Press, 89-113.

Kapleau, Roshi P. (1980) The Three Pillars of Zen: Teaching, Practice, and Enlightenment (revised edn). New York, Doubleday.

Karn, K. and Hayhoe, M. (2000) Memory representations guide targeting eye movements in a natural task. Visual Cognition 7, 673-703.

Kasamatsu, A. and Hirai, T. (1966) An electroencephalographic study on the Zen meditation (zazen). Folia Psychiatrica et Neurologica Japonica 20, 315-36.

Kaiserman-Abramof, I. R., Graybiel, A. M., & Nauta, W. J. (1980). The thalamic projection to cortical area 17 in a congenitally anophthalmic mouse strain. Neuroscience, 5, 41–52.

Kanold, P. O., Kara, P., Reid, R. C., & Shatz, C. J. (2003). Role of subplate neurons in functional maturation of visual cortical columns. Science, 301, 521–525.

Kennedy, H., & Dehay, C. (1988). Functional implications of the anatomical organization of the callosal projections of visual areas V1 and V2 in the macaque monkey. Behav. Brain Res., 29, 225–236.

Kentridge, R.W. and Heywood, C.A. (1999) The status of blindsight. Journal of Consciousness Studies 6(5), 3-11.

Kihlstrom, J.F. (1996) Perception without awareness of what is perceived, learning without awareness of what is learned. In M. Velmans (ed.) The Science of Consciousness. London, Routledge, 23-46.

Kollerstrom, N. (1999) The path of Halley's comet, and Newton's late apprehension of the law of gravity. Annals of Science 56, 331-56.

Kosslyn, S.M. (1980) Image and Mind. Cambridge, MA, Harvard University Press.

Kosslyn, S.M. (1988) Aspects of a cognitive neuroscience of mental imagery. Science 240, 1621-6.

Kinsbourne, M. (1995), 'The intralaminar thalamic nucleii', Consciousness and Cognition, 4.

Kjaer, Troels, Camilla Bertelsen, Paola Piccini, David Brooks, Jorgen Alving, and Hans Lou. "Increased Dopamine Tone during Meditation- Induced Change of Consciousness." Cognitive Brain Research 13, no. 2 (April 2002)

Kölmel HW. 1985. Complex visual hallucinations in the hemianopic field. J Neurol Neurosurg Psychiatry.

Koenig, Harold. "Research on Religion, Spirituality, and Mental Health: A Review." Canadian Journal of Psychiatry 54, no. 5 (May 2009)

Koenig, Harold, ed. Handbook of Religion and Mental Health. San Diego, CA: Academic Press, 1998

Kraepelin E. Psychiatry: A Textbook for Students and Physicians. New York, NY: Science History Publications; 1990.

Lauglin, Charles, John McManus, and Eugene d'Aquili. Brain, Symbol, and Experience. 2nd ed. New York: Columbia University Press, 1992

Lakoff, G. and M. Johnson (1999). Philosophy in the flesh. Basic Books: New York.

LeDoux, J. E. (1996). The emotional brain. New York: Simon & Schuster.

LeDoux, J.E. (1992), 'Emotion and the amygdala', in The Amygdala:

Neurobiological Aspects of Emo- tion, Memory and Mental Dysfunction, ed J.P. Aggleton (New York: Wiley-Liss).

Levin, D.T. and Simons, D.J. (1997) Failure to detect changes to attended objects in motion pictures. Psychonomic Bulletin and Review 4, 501-6.

Levine,J. (1983) Materialism and qualia: the explanatory gap. Pacific Philosophical Quarterly 64, 354-61.

Levine,J. (2001) Purple Haze: The Puzzle of Consciousness. New York, Oxford University Press. Levine, S. (1979) A Gradual Awakening. New York, Doubleday.

Levinson, B.W. (1965) States of awareness during general anaesthesia. British Journal of Anaesthesia 37, 544-6.

Lewicki, P., Czyzewska, M. and Hoffman, H. (1987) Unconscious acquisition of complex procedural knowledge. Journal of Experimental Psychology: Learning, Memory and Cognition 13, 523-30.

Lewicki, P., Hill, T. and Bizot, E. (1988) Acquisition of procedural knowledge about a pattern of stimuli that cannot be articulated. Cognitive Psychology 20, 24-37.

Lewicki, P., Hill, T. and Czyzewska, M. (1992) Nonconscious acquisition of information. American Psychologist 47, 796-801.

Manthey S, Schubotz RI, von Cramon DY (2003). Premotor cortex in observing erroneous action: an fMRI study. Brain Res Cogn Brain Res 15: 296–307.

Mesulam MM, Mufson EJ (1982) Insula of the old world monkey. III: Efferent cortical output and comments on function. J Comp Neurol 212: 38–52.

Naskar, Abhijit. "Homo: A Brief History of Consciousness", 2015

Naskar, Abhijit. "What is Mind?", 2016

Naskar, Abhijit. "Love, God & Neurons: Memoir of A Scientist who found himself by getting lost", 2016

Naskar, Abhijit. "Principia Humanitas", 2017

Naskar, Abhijit. "We Are All Black: A Treatise on Racism", 2017

Naskar, Abhijit. "Either Civilized or Phobic: A Treatise on Homosexuality", 2017

Naskar, Abhijit. "I Am The Thread: My Mission", 2017

Naskar, Abhijit. "The Bengal Tigress: A Treatise on Gender Equality", 2017

Naskar, Abhijit. "Morality Absolute", 2017

Naskar, Abhijit. "Build Bridges not Walls: In the name of Americana", 2018

Naskar, Abhijit. "Fabric of Humanity", 2018

Naskar, Abhijit. "Lives To Serve Before I Sleep", 2019

Naskar, Abhijit. "Citizens of Peace: Beyond the Savagery of Sovereignty", 2019

Naskar, Abhijit. "The Constitution of The United Peoples of Earth", 2019

Naskar, Abhijit. "Neurons Giveth, Neurons Taketh Away | Abhijit Naskar | TEDxIIMRanchi", 2019 https://www.youtube.com/watch?v=B NX-Q0ySm80

Naskar, Abhijit. "Mission Reality", 2019

Naskar, Abhijit. "Operation Justice: To Make A Society That Needs No Law", 2019

Naskar, Abhijit. "Every Generation Needs Caretakers: The Gospel of Patriotism", 2020

Naskar, Abhijit. "Hurricane Humans: Give me accountability, I'll give you peace", 2020

Naskar, Abhijit. "Revolution Indomable", 2020

Naskar, Abhijit. "Servitude is Sanctitude", 2020

Naskar, Abhijit. "Good Scientist: When Science and Service Combine", 2020

Newberg, Andrew, and Jeremy Iversen. "The Neural Basis of the Complex Mental Task of Meditation: Neurotransmitter and Neurochemical Considerations." Medical Hypotheses 61, no. 2 (2003).

Newberg, Andrew. "How God Changes Your Brain: An Introduction to Jewish Neurotheology", CCAR Journal: The Reform Jewish Quarterly, Winter 2016.

Newberg, Andrew, and Stephanie Newberg. "A Neuropsychological

Perspective on Spiritual Development." In Handbook of Spiritual Development in Childhood and Adolescence, edited by Eugene Roehlkepartain, Pamela King, Linda Wagener, and Peter Benson. London: Sage Publications, Inc., 2005

Newberg, Andrew. "The Neurotheology Link An Intersection Between Spirituality and Health", Alternative and Complimentary Therapies, Vol 21 No 1, February 2015.

Newberg, Andrew, Nancy Wintering, Dharma Khalsa, Hannah Roggenkamp, and Mark Waldman. "Meditation Effects on Cognitive Function and Cerebral Blood Flow in Subjects with Memory Loss: A Preliminary Study." Journal of Alzheimer's Disease 20, no. 2 (2010)

Nash, M. (1995), 'Glimpses of the mind', Time.

Nesse RM. Proximate and evolutionary studies of anxiety, stress and depression: synergy at the interface. Neurosci Biobehav Rev. 1999;23:895-903.

Nicolelis, Miguel. (2011) "Beyond Boundaries: The New Neuroscience of Connecting Brains with Machines---and How It Will Change Our Lives", Times Books

O'Hara, K. and Scutt, T. (1996) There is no hard problem of consciousness. Journal of Consciousness Studies 3(4), 290-302, reprinted in J. Shear (ed.) (1997) Explaining Consciousness. Cambridge, MA, MIT Press, 69-82.

O'Regan, J.K. (1992) Solving the "real" mysteries of visual perception: the world as an outside memory. Canadian Journal of Psychology 46, 461-88.

O'Regan, J.K. and Noe, A. (2001) A sensorimotor account of vision and visual consciousness. Behavioral and Brain Sciences 24(5), 883-917.

O'Regan, J.K., Rensink, R.A. and Clark,].]. (1999) Change-blindness as a result of "mudsplashes." Nature 398, 34.

Ornstein, R.E. (1977) The Psychology of Consciousness (2nd edn). New York, Harcourt.

Ornstein, R.E. (1986) The Psychology of Consciousness (3rd edn). New York, Pehguin.

Ornstein, R.E. (1992) The Evolution of Consciousness. New York, Touchstone.

Penfield W, Faulk ME (1955) The insula: further observations on its function. Brain 78: 445– 470.

Penrose, R. (1994), Shadows of the Mind (Oxford: Oxford University Press).

Penrose, R. (1989), The Emperor's New Mind: Concerning Computers, Minds and The Laws of Physics (Oxford: Oxford University Press).

Persinger, "'I would kill in God's name' role of sex, weekly church attendance, report of a religious experience and limbic lability" Perceptual and Motor Skills 1997.

Persinger "Experimental simulation of the God experience" Neurotheology 2003.

Persinger, M. A. (1993b). Personality changes following brain injury as a grief response to the loss of sense of self: Phenomenological themes as indices of local lability and neurocognitive restructuring as psycho- therapy. Psychological Reports, 72

Persinger, Corradini, Clement, Keaney, et al "Neurotheology and its convergence with neuroquantology" NeuroQuantology 2010.

Persinger, Koren and St-Pierre "The electromagnetic induction of mystical and altered states within the laboratory" Journal of Consciousness Exploration and Research 2010.

Persinger "Case report: A prototypical spontaneous 'sensed presence' of a sentient being and concomitant electroencephalographic activity in the clinical laboratory" Neurocase 2008.

Persinger and Saroka "Potential production of Hughlings Jackson's "parasitic consciousness" by physiologically-patterned weak transcerebral magnetic fields: QEEG and source localization" Epilepsy & Behavior 28 (2013).

Persinger. "The neuropsychiatry of paranormal experiences". J Neuropsychiatry Clin Neurosci 2001.

Persinger. "Neuropsychological bases of god beliefs", New York: Praeger, 1987

Persinger. "Temporal lobe epileptic signs and correlative behaviors displayed by normal populations", Journal of General Psychology, 1986

Perry BD, Pollard R. Homeostasis, stress, trauma, and adaptation. A neurodevelopmental view of childhood trauma. Child Adolesc Psychiatr Clin N Am. 1998;7:33.

Paré, D. & Llinás, R. (1995), 'Conscious and preconscious processes as seen from the standpoint of sleep-waking cycle neurophysiology', Neuropsychologia, 33.

P. S. de Laplace. Essai Philosophique sur les Probabilites [1814], in Academy des Sciences, Oeuvres Complotes de Laplace, Vol. 7, Gauthier-Villars, Paris (1886).

Perrett DI, Harries MH, Bevan R, Thomas S, Benson PJ, Mistlin AJ, Chitty AJ, Hietanen JK, Ortega JE (1989) Frameworks of analysis for the neural representation of animate objects and actions. J Exp Bio 146: 87–113.

Phillips ML, Young AW, Senior C, Brammer M, Andrew C, Calder AJ, Bullmore ET, Perrett DI, Rowland D, Williams SC, Gray JA, David AS (1997) A specific neural substrate for perceiving facial expressions of disgust. Nature 389: 495–498.

Phillips ML, Young AW, Scott SK, Calder AJ, Andrew C, Giampietro V, Williams SC, Bullmore ET, Brammer M, Gray JA (1998) Neural responses to facial and vocal expressions of fear and disgust. Proc R Soc Lond B Biol Sci 265: 1809–1817.

Puce A, Perrett D (2003) Electrophysiological and brain imaging of biological motion.

Philosoph Trans Royal Soc Lond, Series B, 358: 435–445.

Ramachandran VS. Behavioral and magnetoencephalographic correlates of plasticity in the adult human brain. Proc Natl Acad Sci USA 1993; 90: 10413–20.

Ramachandran VS. Phantom limbs, neglect syndromes, repressed memories, and Freudian psychology. Int Rev Neurobiol 1994; 37: 291–333.

Ramachandran VS. Plasticity and functional recovery in neurology. Clin Med 2005; 5: 368–73.

Ramachandran VS, Hirstein W. The perception of phantom limbs. The D. O. Hebb lecture. Brain 1998; 121: 1603–30.

Ramachandran VS, Rogers-Ramachandran D, Cobb S. Touching the phantom limb. Nature 1995; 377: 489–90.

Ramachandran VS, Rogers-Ramachandran D. Phantom limbs and neural plasticity. Arch Neurol 2000; 57: 317–20.

Ramachandran VS, Rogers-Ramachandran D. It's all done with mirrors. Sci Am Mind 2007; 18: 16–9.

Ramachandran VS, Rogers-Ramachandran D. Sensations referred to a patient's phantom arm from another subjects intact arm: perceptual correlates of mirror neurons. Med Hypotheses 2008; 70: 1233–4.

Ramachandran VS, Rogers-Ramachandran D, Stewart M. Perceptual correlates of massive cortical reorganization. Science 1992; 258: 1159–60.

Rizzolatti G, Craighero L (2004) The mirror-neuron system. Annu Rev Neurosci 27: 169–192.

Rizzolatti G, Fogassi L, Gallese V (2001) Neurophysiological mechanisms underlying the understanding and imitation of action. Nature Rev Neurosci 2:661–670.

Rock I, Victor J. Vision and touch: an experimentally created conflict between the two senses. Science 1964; 143: 594–6.

Rose'n B, Lundborg G. Training with a mirror in rehabilitation of the hand. Scand J Plast Reconstr Surg Hand Surg 2005; 39: 104–8.

Royet JP, Plailly J, Delon-Martin C, Kareken DA, Segebarth C (2003) fMRI of emotional responses to odors: influence of hedonic valence and judgment, handedness, and gender. Neuroimage 20: 713–728.

Rozin R Haidt J and McCauley CR (2000) Disgust. In: Lewis M, Haviland-Jones JM (eds) Handbook of Emotion. 2nd Edition. Guilford Press, New York, pp 637–653.

Saxe R, Carey S, Kanwisher N (2004) Understanding other minds: linking developmental psychology and functional neuroimaging. Annu Rev Psychol 55: 87–124.

S. J. Russell and P. Norvig, Artificial intelligence: a modern approach (3rd edition): Prentice Hall, 2009.

Schienle A, Stark R, Walter B, Blecker C, Ott U, Kirsch P, Sammer G, Vaitl D (2002) The insula is not specifically involved in disgust processing: an fMRI study. Neuroreport 13: 2023–2026.

Showers MJC, Lauer EW (1961) Somatovisceral motor patterns in the insula. J Comp Neurol 117: 107–115.

Singer T, Seymour B, O'Doherty J, Kaube H, Dolan RJ, Frith CD (2004) Empathy for pain involves the affective but not the sensory components of pain. Science 303: 1157–1162.

Smith A (1759) The theory of moral sentiments (ed. 1976). Clarendon Press, Oxford.

S. N. Bose (1924). "Plancks Gesetz und Lichtquantenhypothese". Zeitschrift für Physik. 26 (1): 178–181.

Sprengelmeyer R, Rausch M, Eysel UT, Przuntek H (1998) Neural structures associated with recognition of facial expressions of basic emotions Proc R Soc Lond B Biol Sci 265: 1927–1931.

Strafella AP, Paus T (2000) Modulation of cortical excitability during action observation: a transcranial magnetic stimulation study. NeuroReport 11: 2289–2292.

Schilling, Vincent. 2017, indian country today

Stein, Stephen K. 2017, The Sea in World History: Exploration, Travel, and Trade

Simonsen R (2015) Eating for the future: veganism and the challenge of in vitro meat. In: Stapleton P, Byers A (Hg). Biopolitics and utopia. Palgrave Macmillan, New York (2015), S 167–190

Tanaka K (1996) Inferotemporal cortex and object vision. Ann Rev Neurosci. 19: 109–140.

Tesla N. "My Inventions", 1919

T. R. Society, "Machine learning: the power and promise of computers that learn by example," ed. The Royal Society, 2017.

Tomasello M, Call J (1997) Primate cognition. Oxford University Press, Oxford.

Tremblay C, Robert M, Pascual-Leone A, Lepore F, Nguyen DK, Carmant L, Bouthillier A, Theoret H (2004) Action observation and execution: intracranial recordings in a human subject. Neurology. 63: 937–938.

Umilta MA, Kohler E, Gallese V, Fogassi L, Fadiga L, Keysers C, Rizzolatti G (2001) "I know what you are doing": a neurophysiological study. Neuron 32: 91–101.

Von Wright G.H., (1963), Norm and Action. A Logical Inquiry, Routledge & Kegan Paul, London.

Von Wright G.H., (1976), "Determinism and the Study of Man", in Essays on Explanation and Understanding, ed. by J. Manninen and R. Tuomela, Reidel, Dordrecht.

Von Wright G.H., (1977), "What is Humanism?", The Lindlay Lecture, University of Arkansas, Lawrence, Kansas.

Von Wright G.H., (1979), "Humanism and the Humanities", in Philosophy and Grammar, ed. by S. Kanger and S. Öhman, Reidel, Dordrecht, pp. 1-16. Reprinted in von Wright (1993).

Von Wright G.H., (1980), Freedom and Determination, North-Holland Publishing Co., Amsterdam.

Von Wright G.H., (1985), Of Human Freedom, The Tanner Lectures on Human Values,

Vol. VI, ed. by S. M. McMurrin, University of Utah Press, Salt Lake City, pp. 107-70. Reprinted in von Wright (1998).

Von Wright G.H., (1993), The Tree of Knowledge and Other Essays, Brill, Leiden.

Von Wright G.H., (1997), "Progress: Fact and Fiction", in The Idea of Progress, ed. by A. Burgen et al., W. de Gruyter, Berlin, pp. 1-18.

Von Wright G.H., (1998), In the Shadow of Descartes: Essays in the Philosophy of Mind, Kluwer, Dordrecht.